MOVIE SONGS FOR TWO

Arrangements by Mark Phillips

ISBN 978-1-5400-3719-0

HAL•LEONARD®

Visit Hal Leonard Online at
www.halleonard.com

Contact us:
Hal Leonard
7777 West Bluemound Road
Milwaukee, WI 53213
Email: info@halleonard.com

In Europe, contact:
Hal Leonard Europe Limited
42 Wigmore Street
Marylebone, London, W1U 2RN
Email: info@halleonardeurope.com

In Australia, contact:
Hal Leonard Australia Pty. Ltd.
4 Lentara Court
Cheltenham, Victoria, 3192 Australia
Email: info@halleonard.com.au

BABY ELEPHANT WALK

from the Paramount Picture HATARI!

By HENRY MANCINI

TROMBONES

Moderately, with humor

THE CANDY MAN
from WILLY WONKA AND THE CHOCOLATE FACTORY

TROMBONES

Words and Music by LESLIE BRICUSSE
and ANTHONY NEWLEY

CITY OF STARS

from LA LA LAND

TROMBONES

Music by JUSTIN HURWITZ
Lyrics by BENJ PASEK and JUSTIN PAUL

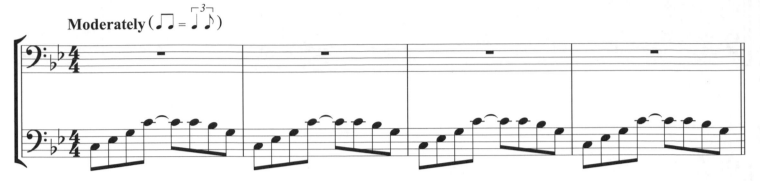

CUPS
(When I'm Gone)
from the Motion Picture Soundtrack PITCH PERFECT

TROMBONES

Words and Music by A.P. CARTER,
LUISA GERSTEIN and HELOISE TUNSTALL-BEHRTENS

Moderately fast

17

20

23

Fine

27

30

D.S. al Fine

FOOTLOOSE

Theme from the Paramount Motion Picture FOOTLOOSE

TROMBONES

Words by DEAN PITCHFORD
Music by KENNY LOGGINS

Fast

HALLELUJAH

featured in the DreamWorks Motion Picture SHREK

TROMBONES

Words and Music by
LEONARD COHEN

Moderately slow, in 2

HAPPY

from DESPICABLE ME 2

Words and Music by
PHARRELL WILLIAMS

TROMBONES

I WILL ALWAYS LOVE YOU

featured in THE BODYGUARD

TROMBONES

Words and Music by
DOLLY PARTON

Moderately slow

JAILHOUSE ROCK

from JAILHOUSE ROCK

TROMBONES

Words and Music by JERRY LEIBER
and MIKE STOLLER

Moderately fast Rock

MIA & SEBASTIAN'S THEME

from LA LA LAND

TROMBONES

Music by JUSTIN HURWITZ

Moderately slow

MRS. ROBINSON

from THE GRADUATE

Words and Music by
PAUL SIMON

TROMBONES

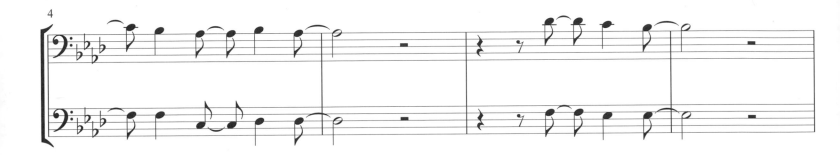

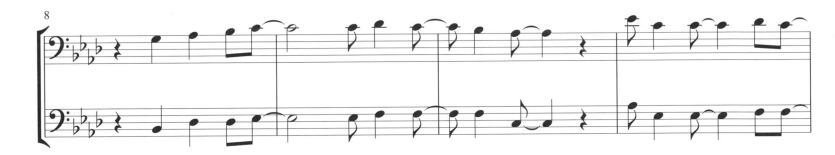

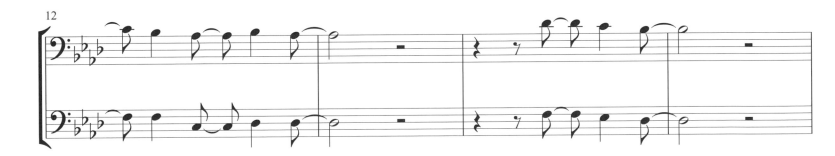

To Coda

D.S. al Coda

CODA

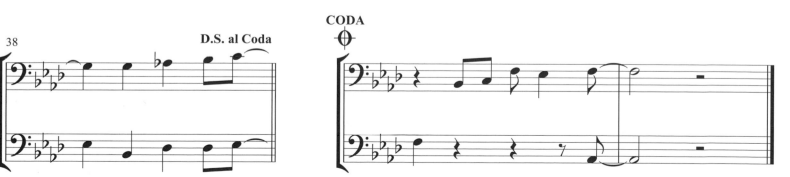

MOON RIVER

from the Paramount Picture BREAKFAST AT TIFFANY'S

TROMBONES

Words by JOHNNY MERCER
Music by HENRY MANCINI

Moderately

THE PINK PANTHER

from THE PINK PANTHER

By HENRY MANCINI

TROMBONES

Moderately, in 4

PUTTIN' ON THE RITZ

from the Motion Picture PUTTIN' ON THE RITZ
featured in YOUNG FRANKENSTEIN

TROMBONES

Words and Music by
IRVING BERLIN

THE RAINBOW CONNECTION

from THE MUPPET MOVIE

TROMBONES

Words and Music by PAUL WILLIAMS
and KENNETH L. ASCHER

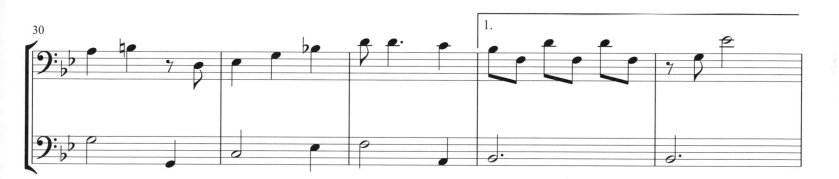

RAINDROPS KEEP FALLIN' ON MY HEAD

from BUTCH CASSIDY AND THE SUNDANCE KID

TROMBONES

Lyrics by HAL DAVID
Music by BURT BACHARACH

ROCK AROUND THE CLOCK

featured in the Motion Picture AMERICAN GRAFFITI
featured in the Motion Picture BLACKBOARD JUNGLE

TROMBONES

Words and Music by MAX C. FREEDMAN
and JIMMY DeKNIGHT

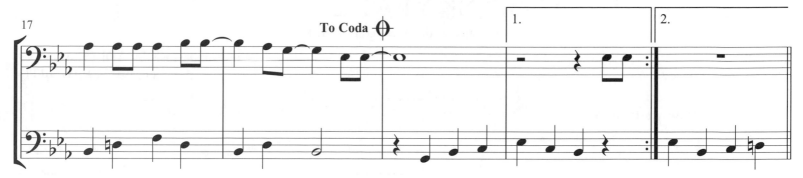

SKYFALL

from the Motion Picture SKYFALL

TROMBONES

Words and Music by ADELE ADKINS
and PAUL EPWORTH

Moderately slow

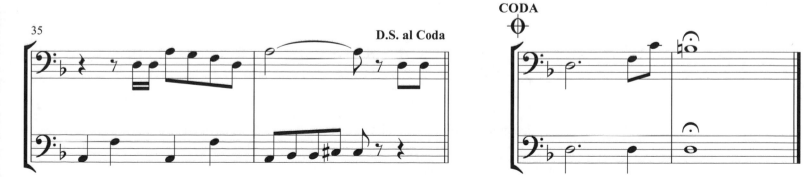

STAYIN' ALIVE

from the Motion Picture SATURDAY NIGHT FEVER

TROMBONES

Words and Music by BARRY GIBB,
ROBIN GIBB and MAURICE GIBB

Moderately, in 2

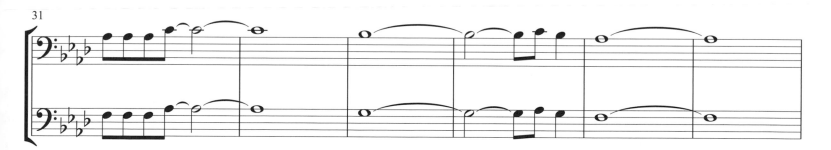

THAT'S AMORÉ
(That's Love)
from the Paramount Picture THE CADDY
featured in the Motion Picture MOONSTRUCK
featured in ENCHANTED

Words by JACK BROOKS
Music by HARRY WARREN

TROMBONES

Fast Waltz

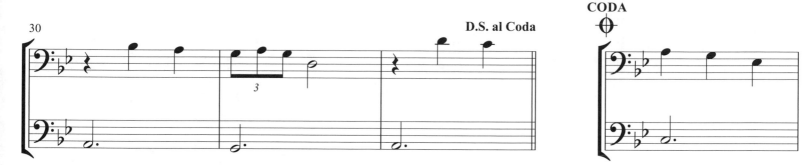

D.S. al Coda

CODA

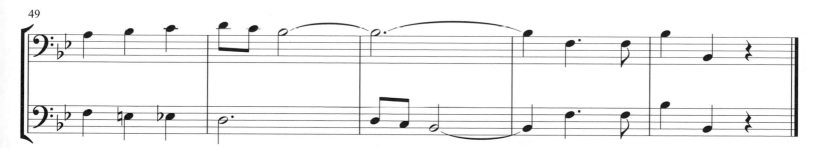

TIME WARP

from THE ROCKY HORROR PICTURE SHOW

TROMBONES

Words and Music by
RICHARD O'BRIEN

Fast Rock

UNCHAINED MELODY

from the Motion Picture UNCHAINED
featured in the Motion Picture GHOST

Lyric by HY ZARET
Music by ALEX NORTH

TROMBONES

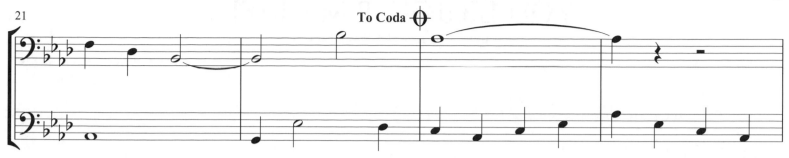

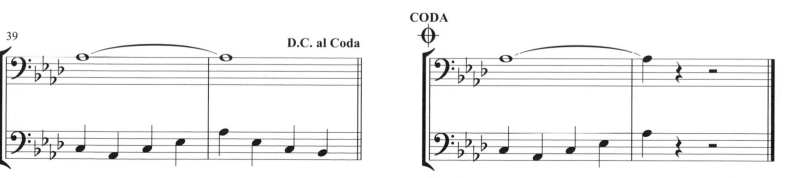

YOU LIGHT UP MY LIFE

from YOU LIGHT UP MY LIFE

Words and Music by
JOSEPH BROOKS

TROMBONES

HAL·LEONARD INSTRUMENTAL PLAY-ALONG

Your favorite songs are arranged just for solo instrumentalists with this outstanding series. Each book includes great full-accompaniment play-along audio so you can sound just like a pro! Check out **www.halleonard.com** to see all the titles available.

The Beatles

All You Need Is Love • Blackbird • Day Tripper • Eleanor Rigby • Get Back • Here, There and Everywhere • Hey Jude • I Will • Let It Be • Lucy in the Sky with Diamonds • Ob-La-Di, Ob-La-Da • Penny Lane • Something • Ticket to Ride • Yesterday.

_____ 00225330	Flute	$14.99
_____ 00225331	Clarinet	$14.99
_____ 00225332	Alto Sax	$14.99
_____ 00225333	Tenor Sax	$14.99
_____ 00225334	Trumpet	$14.99
_____ 00225335	Horn	$14.99
_____ 00225336	Trombone	$14.99
_____ 00225337	Violin	$14.99
_____ 00225338	Viola	$14.99
_____ 00225339	Cello	$14.99

Chart Hits

All About That Bass • All of Me • Happy • Radioactive • Roar • Say Something • Shake It Off • A Sky Full of Stars • Someone like You • Stay with Me • Thinking Out Loud • Uptown Funk.

_____ 00146207	Flute	$12.99
_____ 00146208	Clarinet	$12.99
_____ 00146209	Alto Sax	$12.99
_____ 00146210	Tenor Sax	$12.99
_____ 00146211	Trumpet	$12.99
_____ 00146212	Horn	$12.99
_____ 00146213	Trombone	$12.99
_____ 00146214	Violin	$12.99
_____ 00146215	Viola	$12.99
_____ 00146216	Cello	$12.99

Disney Greats

Arabian Nights • Hawaiian Roller Coaster Ride • It's a Small World • Look Through My Eyes • Yo Ho (A Pirate's Life for Me) • and more.

_____ 00841934	Flute	$12.99
_____ 00841935	Clarinet	$12.99
_____ 00841936	Alto Sax	$12.99
_____ 00841937	Tenor Sax	$12.95
_____ 00841938	Trumpet	$12.99
_____ 00841939	Horn	$12.99
_____ 00841940	Trombone	$12.99
_____ 00841941	Violin	$12.99
_____ 00841942	Viola	$12.99
_____ 00841943	Cello	$12.99
_____ 00842078	Oboe	$12.99

The Greatest Showman

Come Alive • From Now On • The Greatest Show • A Million Dreams • Never Enough • The Other Side • Rewrite the Stars • This Is Me • Tightrope.

_____ 00277389	Flute	$14.99
_____ 00277390	Clarinet	$14.99
_____ 00277391	Alto Sax	$14.99
_____ 00277392	Tenor Sax	$14.99
_____ 00277393	Trumpet	$14.99
_____ 00277394	Horn	$14.99
_____ 00277395	Trombone	$14.99
_____ 00277396	Violin	$14.99
_____ 00277397	Viola	$14.99
_____ 00277398	Cello	$14.99

Movie and TV Music

The Avengers • Doctor Who XI • Downton Abbey • Game of Thrones • Guardians of the Galaxy • Hawaii Five-O • Married Life • Rey's Theme (from *Star Wars: The Force Awakens*) • The X-Files • and more.

_____ 00261807	Flute	$12.99
_____ 00261808	Clarinet	$12.99
_____ 00261809	Alto Sax	$12.99
_____ 00261810	Tenor Sax	$12.99
_____ 00261811	Trumpet	$12.99
_____ 00261812	Horn	$12.99
_____ 00261813	Trombone	$12.99
_____ 00261814	Violin	$12.99
_____ 00261815	Viola	$12.99
_____ 00261816	Cello	$12.99

12 Pop Hits

Believer • Can't Stop the Feeling • Despacito • It Ain't Me • Look What You Made Me Do • Million Reasons • Perfect • Send My Love (To Your New Lover) • Shape of You • Slow Hands • Too Good at Goodbyes • What About Us.

_____ 00261790	Flute	$12.99
_____ 00261791	Clarinet	$12.99
_____ 00261792	Alto Sax	$12.99
_____ 00261793	Tenor Sax	$12.99
_____ 00261794	Trumpet	$12.99
_____ 00261795	Horn	$12.99
_____ 00261796	Trombone	$12.99
_____ 00261797	Violin	$12.99
_____ 00261798	Viola	$12.99
_____ 00261799	Cello	$12.99

Songs from Frozen, Tangled and Enchanted

Do You Want to Build a Snowman? • For the First Time in Forever • Happy Working Song • I See the Light • In Summer • Let It Go • Mother Knows Best • That's How You Know • True Love's First Kiss • When Will My Life Begin • and more.

_____ 00126921	Flute	$14.99
_____ 00126922	Clarinet	$14.99
_____ 00126923	Alto Sax	$14.99
_____ 00126924	Tenor Sax	$14.99
_____ 00126925	Trumpet	$14.99
_____ 00126926	Horn	$14.99
_____ 00126927	Trombone	$14.99
_____ 00126928	Violin	$14.99
_____ 00126929	Viola	$14.99
_____ 00126930	Cello	$14.99

Top Hits

Adventure of a Lifetime • Budapest • Die a Happy Man • Ex's & Oh's • Fight Song • Hello • Let It Go • Love Yourself • One Call Away • Pillowtalk • Stitches • Writing's on the Wall.

_____ 00171073	Flute	$12.99
_____ 00171074	Clarinet	$12.99
_____ 00171075	Alto Sax	$12.99
_____ 00171106	Tenor Sax	$12.99
_____ 00171107	Trumpet	$12.99
_____ 00171108	Horn	$12.99
_____ 00171109	Trombone	$12.99
_____ 00171110	Violin	$12.99
_____ 00171111	Viola	$12.99
_____ 00171112	Cello	$12.99

Wicked

As Long As You're Mine • Dancing Through Life • Defying Gravity • For Good • I'm Not That Girl • Popular • The Wizard and I • and more.

_____ 00842236	Flute	$12.99
_____ 00842237	Clarinet	$12.99
_____ 00842238	Alto Saxophone	$12.99
_____ 00842239	Tenor Saxophone	$11.95
_____ 00842240	Trumpet	$12.99
_____ 00842241	Horn	$12.99
_____ 00842242	Trombone	$12.99
_____ 00842243	Violin	$12.99
_____ 00842244	Viola	$12.99
_____ 00842245	Cello	$12.99

Prices, contents, and availability subject to change without notice.
Disney characters and Artwork ™ & © 2018 Disney

HAL·LEONARD®